Drew Brees

by Kathy Allen

Consultant: Barry Wilner
AP Football Writer

New York, New York

Credits

Cover and Title Page, © David Drapkin/AP Images and Bill Feig/AP Images; 4, © Matt Brown/
Icon SMI; 5, © Denis Poroy/AP Images; 6, © Bill Haber/AP Images; 7, © Brad Schloss/
Icon SMI; 8, © AP Images; 9, © Action Sports Photography/Shutterstock Images; 10, ©
Seth Poppel/Yearbook Library; 11, © Ralph Barrera/American-Statesman/WPN; 12, ©
Stephen P. Goodwin/Shutterstock Images; 13, © Taylor Johnson/Austin American-Statesman;
14, © Michael Conroy/AP Images; 15, © Todd Warshaw/Icon SMI; 16, © Reed Saxon/
AP Images; 17, © Lenny Ignelzi/AP Images; 18, © Denis Poroy/AP Images; 19, © Charles
Baus/Icon SMI; 20, © Joe Seer/Shutterstock Images; 21, © Icon SMI; 22, © Action Sports
Photography/Shutterstock Images.

Publisher: Kenn Goin
Senior Editor: Joyce Tavolacci
Creative Director: Spencer Brinker
Photo Researcher: Arnold Ringstad
Design: Emily Love

Library of Congress Cataloging-in-Publication Data

Allen, Kathy.
  Drew Brees / by Kathy Allen.
      p. cm. (Football stars up close)
  Includes bibliographical references and index.
  ISBN 978-1-61772-716-0 (library binding) – ISBN 1-61772-716-4 (library binding)
 1. Brees, Drew, 1979–Juvenile literature. 2. Football players–United States–Biography–
Juvenile literature. I. Title.
  GV939.B695A55 2013
  796.332092–dc23
  [B]
                                    2012037977

For more information, write to Bearport Publishing Company, Inc., 45 West 21st Street, Suite
3B, New York, New York 10010. Printed in the United States of America.

10 9 8 7 6 5 4 3 2

Contents

The End of a Career?

It was the last game of the 2005 **NFL** season. Drew Brees lay injured on the field. The San Diego Chargers **quarterback** had just been knocked to the ground by a huge 325-pound (147 kg) Denver Broncos player. Pain shot through badly torn muscles in Drew's right shoulder. As he got up and walked off the field, some wondered whether his throwing arm would ever be the same again.

Drew gets ready to throw the ball with his right arm earlier in the 2005 season.

Drew (#9) is helped off the field after injuring his shoulder.

Drew had been the quarterback for the Chargers since 2001. He led the team to an impressive 12–4 record in 2004.

Comeback Quarterback

To fix his shoulder, Drew underwent **surgery** and months of painful **physical therapy**. Because of his hard work and determination, his shoulder healed. Drew then decided it was time to change teams. He signed with the New Orleans Saints to be their new **starting** quarterback. In his first game with the new team, he thrilled Saints fans with his strong arm and precise **passing**. Thanks to Drew, the Saints won 19–14! The season was just getting started, and so was the comeback quarterback.

Drew holds up his new Saints jersey.

Drew throws the ball in his first regular season game with the Saints.

The Saints started 2006 with a new head coach, Sean Payton. Saints fans hoped the new quarterback and new coach would help the team win more games.

Sports Family

It's no surprise Drew grew up to be a great athlete. As a child, he was surrounded by sports. He was born on January 15, 1979, in Austin, Texas. His grandfather was a high school football coach and his uncle a quarterback. Drew spent many days at home playing football with his younger brother, Reid.

Drew Brees was named after Drew Pearson, a  for the Dallas Cowboys who played from 1973 to 1983.

Drew Pearson

Playing catch with his brother as a child helped Drew become a great passer as an adult.

High School

When it was time for high school, Drew joined the football team. In his junior year, he became starting quarterback and led the team to ten wins and no losses. His quick throws and fast moves resulted in big gains on the field. Drew played even better in his senior year, leading his team to a state **championship** in 1996.

Drew's yearbook photo, senior year

Drew launches a football in a high school game.

In his senior year of high school, Drew's team won all 16 of the games it played.

Small Wonder

Although Drew was a great high school quarterback, he was shorter and lighter than other top players. To make up for this, Drew was extra fast on his feet and always knew where to run and pass the ball. Because of his small size, many colleges did not ask him to join their teams. However, Purdue University in Indiana saw Drew's talent and made him an offer. Drew gladly accepted.

Purdue University in Indiana

Though Drew was smaller than other high school players, he was still a star quarterback.

Drew threw for an amazing 3,528 yards (3,226 m) and 31 touchdowns in his senior year of high school.

College Standout

In 1998, Drew's second year at Purdue, he became the starting quarterback. He wowed his fans when he broke the school record for the most touchdown passes. Drew had an incredible ability to break through the opposing team's defense and help score touchdowns. Despite his size, he had proven he could shine on the field.

Drew smiles after winning a 2000 game against Ohio State.

Drew looks for an open player to throw the ball to in a 1999 game against Penn State.

In 2000, Drew earned the Maxwell Award. This is an award given by sports reporters and coaches to the best college football player in the country.

NFL Starter

Because of his success in college, the San Diego Chargers picked Drew to join their team in 2001. He failed to bring the team to the **playoffs** in 2002 or 2003. As a result, in 2004, the Chargers thought about replacing Drew with another quarterback. However, they decided to give Drew one last chance to lead the team to victory. Could Drew show them that he deserved to keep his job as the starter?

Drew practices his footwork while getting ready for the 2004 season.

Although Drew started all 16 games in 2002, he led the Chargers to only eight wins.

Drew during his first practice with the Chargers

17

From Playoffs to Injury

Drew quickly showed that he deserved to keep his job. In 2004, Drew led the Chargers to the playoffs! The next season he passed for an impressive 3,576 yards (3,270 m), a personal record. However, it was in the last game of the 2005 season that Drew injured his shoulder and then left the Chargers. A few months later, the Saints gave Drew a second chance at success when they asked him to join their team. Drew knew if he worked extra hard, he could become a top player once again—and he was right.

Drew speaks with a Chargers coach during a 2005 game.

Drew prepares to throw a ball during a 2004 game.

The doctor who treated Drew's shoulder thought it was unlikely he would ever return to the NFL at all, let alone become a superstar quarterback.

Comeback Champion

In 2006, his first year with his new team, Drew carried the Saints to the playoffs. In the 2009 season, he led his team all the way to the **Super Bowl**. Drew threw a record 32 **completions** in the game, and the Saints won 31–17! Through hard work, willpower, and pinpoint passing, Drew Brees had proven himself to be a comeback champion.

Drew and his teammates show off their Super Bowl championship rings.

Drew holds up his team's trophy after winning the Super Bowl.

In 2003, Drew started a charity called the Brees Dream Foundation. It raises money for children's hospitals and the American Cancer Society.

Drew's Life and Career

⭐ **January 15, 1979**   Drew Brees is born in Austin, Texas.

⭐ **1996**   Drew leads his high school football team to a state championship.

⭐ **1998**   Drew begins playing as starting quarterback for Purdue University.

⭐ **2000**   Drew wins the Maxwell Award.

⭐ **2001**   The San Diego Chargers select Drew to play for them.

⭐ **2003**   Drew starts the Brees Dream Foundation.

⭐ **2004**   Drew brings the Chargers to the playoffs.

⭐ **2005**   Drew injures his right shoulder in the last game of the season.

⭐ **2006**   Drew leaves the Chargers and is signed by the New Orleans Saints.

⭐ **2010**   Drew and the New Orleans Saints win the Super Bowl.

Glossary

championship (CHAM-pee-uhn-ship)
a contest or final game of a series that decides which team will be the winner

completions (kom-PLEE-shunz)
throws by quarterbacks that are caught by receivers

NFL (EN-EFF-ELL)
letters standing for the National Football League, which includes 32 teams

passing (PASS-ing)
throwing the ball to another player

physical therapy
(FIZ-uh-kuhl THER-uh-pee)
the use of exercise and equipment to heal an injury to the body

playoffs (PLAY-awfss)
the games held after the end of the regular football season that determine which two teams will compete in the Super Bowl

quarterback (KWOR-tur-bak)
a football player who leads the offense, the part of a team that moves the ball forward

starting (START-ting)
being the coach's first choice to play in a game

Super Bowl (SOO-pur BOHL)
the final championship game in the NFL playoffs, played on the first Sunday in February

surgery (SUR-jur-ee)
the part of medical science that treats injuries by fixing parts of the body

touchdowns (TUHCH-*douns*)
scores of six points, made by getting the ball across the other team's goal line

wide receiver (WIDE ri-SEE-vur)
a player whose job it is to catch passes

Index

Bibliography

Brees, Drew, with Chris Fabry. *Coming Back Stronger*. Carol Stream,
    IL: Tyndale (2010).

Drew Brees's Official Web Site: www.drewbrees.com

Official Site of the New Orleans Saints: www.neworleanssaints.com

Read More

Artell, Mike. *Drew Brees: Football Superstar (Superstar Athletes)*.
    Mankato, MN: Capstone (2012).

Sandler, Michael. *Drew Brees and the New Orleans Saints: Super
    Bowl XLIV (Super Bowl Superstars)*. New York: Bearport (2011).

Torsiello, David P. *Read About Drew Brees (I Like Sports Stars!)*.
    Berkeley Heights, NJ: Enslow Elementary (2011).

Learn More Online

To learn more about Drew Brees, visit
www.bearportpublishing.com/FootballStarsUpClose